Contents

D1740360

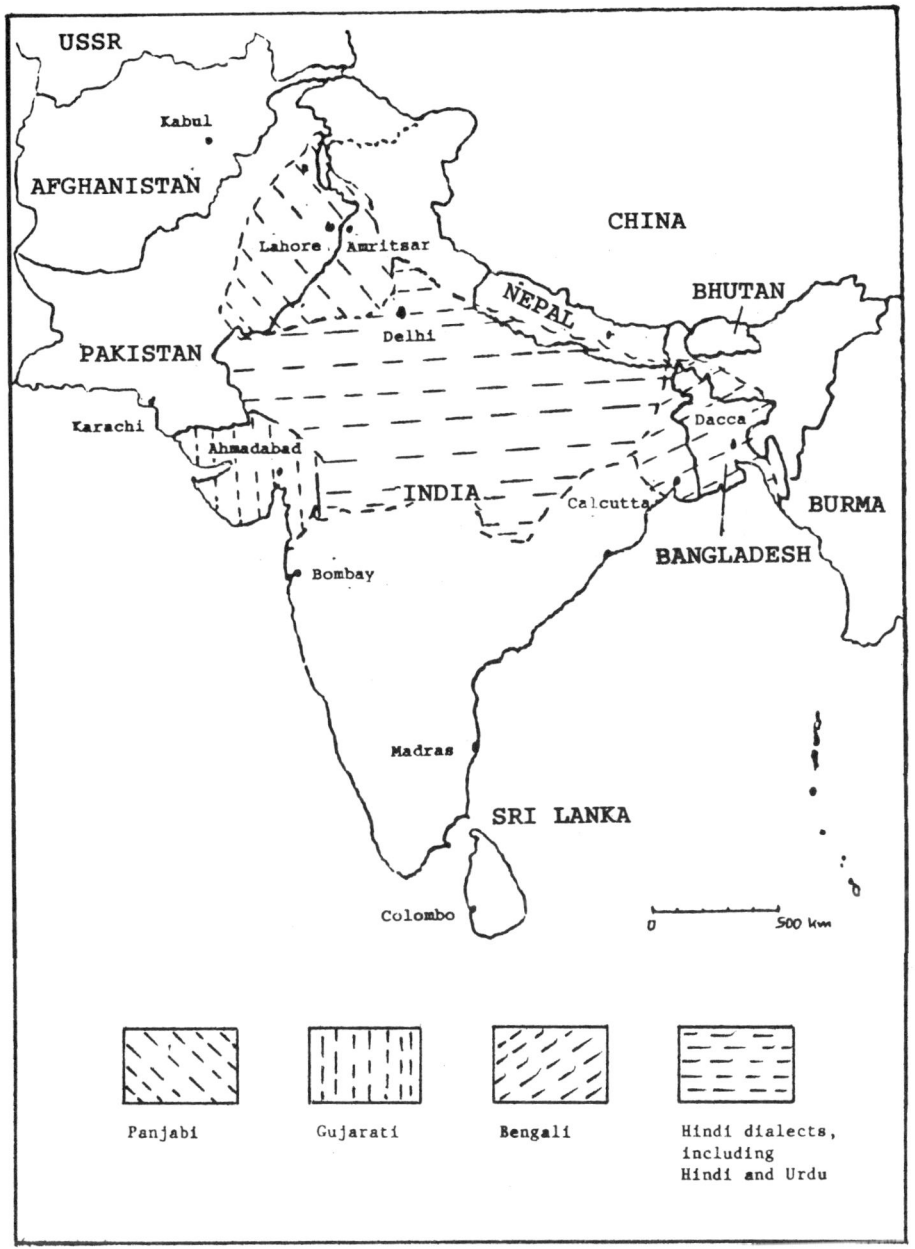

The states of South Asia, showing the regions where the
five main languages discussed in this book are widely
spoken as mother tongues (not necessarily corresponding
to the official languages of these states).

Foreword and acknowledgements

This book is an introduction to the subject of the principal languages spoken by people of South Asian origin living in Britain. It is intended to assist people in Britain whose work involves them with speakers of these languages in multi-ethnic areas of the country, and who are hoping to acquire some knowledge of the languages or at least to understand some of the linguistic habits of their speakers. It is descriptive and practical in approach, not seeking to teach the languages themselves but to give linguistic, geographical and historical background information which may lead to a deeper appreciation of the languages and their speakers.

It begins by outlining the relationship to Western European languages of the major languages of Pakistan, Northern India and Bangladesh (Chapter 1), then describes some general characteristics of the grammatical structure, sounds, scripts and vocabulary of these languages (Chapter 2). The main languages spoken among communities of South Asian origin who have migrated to Britain, i.e. Panjabi, Gujarati, Bengali, Urdu and Hindi, are discussed in detail, with information on aspects such as regional origin and present status within South Asia, and the connections between religious affiliation and choice of script (Chapter 3). The position of these languages in Britain and the current debate on the inclusion of community languages in the mainstream school curriculum are briefly discussed in Chapter 4.

To keep the text as readable as possible, all 'footnote'-type information together with all bibliographical references and suggestions for further reading have been placed in the 'Notes and references' section at the back, indicated by numbers in parenthesis in the main text. These may be followed up at will; they are not essential to the understanding of the subject as treated in this book.

The writer wishes to thank members of the former Linguistic Minorities Project, University of London Institute of Education (Director: Dr Verity Saifullah Khan), in particular Marilyn Martin Jones, Euan Reid and Greg Smith. Thanks are also due to Xavier Couillaud of Language Information Network Coordination, and to June Geach of the Centre for Information on Language Teaching and Research; also to Dr R S McGregor, Lecturer in Hindi at Cambridge University, and especially to Mr R Russell, former Reader in Urdu at the School of Oriental and African Studies, London University, for their generous help in reading the first draft of this book and making many valuable suggestions and corrections. The particular sections relating to Panjabi, Gujarati and Bengali were also read by Dr C Shackle, Dr I M P Raeside and Dr J Boulton respectively, all of the School of Oriental and African Studies. Their assistance must also be acknow-

1

ledged. Any inaccuracies in the text remain the responsibility of the writer.

(An earlier version of this book appeared as a contribution to 'Polyglot', Volume 4, No. 1. 1982.)

Introduction

This book is about the languages of those people settled in Britain whose origins are in the Indian Subcontinent. This is the geographical region comprising the present-day states of Pakistan, India, Nepal, Bhutan, Bangladesh and Sri Lanka; it is also referred to as South Asia. For our purposes, however, the terms Indian Subcontinent and South Asia will be taken to refer simply to Bangladesh, India and Pakistan, the three countries from which large numbers of people have migrated to Britain. (We will not distinguish between those who migrated to Britain directly and those who came to Britain indirectly, by way of previous settlement in East Africa, the Carribean, Mauritius or elsewhere.) The focus will be on the languages whose speakers are most prominent numerically in Britain, namely Panjabi, Gujarati, Bengali, Urdu and Hindi. Certainly other South Asian languages are spoken by settlers in Britain (e.g. Tamil, Malayalam, Marathi), but these have relatively small numbers of speakers in Britain and can receive only passing reference in what follows.

'Outsiders' encounter several difficulties when they try to understand the South Asian language situation for the first time. The aim of this book, therefore, is to present information which will clarify these problems and lead to a better understanding of the linguistic and cultural characteristics of people of South Asian origin in Britain. The sources of some common misunderstandings and misconceptions are outlined below:

1. One difficulty relates to the actual names of the various languages: the word for the people who speak a language, the name of the language itself and the name of its writing system are easily confused. For example, many people from the Panjab (Panjabis) write their language in the Gurmukhi script; the language itself is called Panjabi. Also, Hindi is the name of a language and has no associated 'people' name; the word Hindu refers to a religious, not a linguistic, classification. Despite the confusing similarity of the two words, there is no necessary correspondence between Hindi (speaking) and Hindu.

2. Confusion also arises from the different possible ways of classifying people of South Asian origin; besides language, these include country of origin, religion, and the particular writing system the people are most familiar with. These classifications correspond to each other in some cases, but not in others. Thus, despite a common spoken language, Panjabi speakers in Britain form two distinct groupings on the basis of country of origin, religion and script.

3. There is an apparent extravagance of scripts - one for each

of the five languages we are dealing with here. However, with the exception of the Perso-Arabic script which is used for writing Urdu, all the South Asian scripts derive from a common source – they are variations on a single theme, so to speak. The underlying system of letter-sound correspondence is the same in all cases.

4. Similarly, the sheer number of languages within a single country such as India is perplexing for many monoglot English-speaking people. The relative status of the different languages in a multilingual political entity can be difficult for outsiders to appreciate. Within India alone, all five languages treated in this booklet are of major importance. India is of course renowned (some might say 'notorious') as an area of linguistic diversity. For example, Taya Zinkin (India, OUP 1964) refers to "over 800 languages and dialects" as an instance of the "extraordinary diversity of India" (p 10). It should be remembered, however, that India is approximately the size of Europe (excluding the USSR); if all the European languages, not only national languages but also regional and other minority languages and dialects, were taken into account, then the linguistic picture which emerged in Europe would not be so very different from that of India. The point will be made throughout this book that, in contrast to the predominantly monoglot nature of the English-speaking countries, bi- and multi-lingualism is the norm in South Asia, and has been so throughout history.

5. Finally, the realisation that there is such a thing as an 'Indo-European' language family might lead to the expectation that Indian (and by extension South Asian) languages should be visibly related to European ones, including of course English; it is a disappointment when resemblances are hard if not impossible to spot. We will look briefly in the first Chapter at some of the correspondences which <u>can</u> be found between Hindi, Panjabi etc on the one hand and English, French etc on the other, and at how these correspondences arose. We will do this not so much for any linguistic interest in the matter, but rather to stress the common ground between English and the major languages of South Asian settlers in Britain, to counterbalance the more general tendency which stresses the <u>differences</u> between minority and majority sections of society.

In outline, then, in this book we will look firstly at the historical connections which have been shown to exist between certain South Asian languages and English and many other European languages; secondly, at some historical and grammatical characteristics common to all five languages – Urdu and Hindi, Panjabi, Bengali and Gujarati; thirdly, at each of these languages individually – in terms of their importance and function in the countries of the Subcontinent, including an explanation, where appropriate, of the religion-script-language interrelationships; and finally at the status and role of these languages in Britain today, especially in institutional terms (education, media etc).

1. The Indo-European connection

1.1 Language kinship

The concept of historical relationships between languages is fairly well-known today. For readers who may not be familiar with it, the main point is that languages change during the course of time, in matters of grammar, vocabulary and sounds. Further, a particular language will change in different ways if the people who speak it become separated into groups which cease to be in regular communication with each other. An example of this would be the development of the English language in America which began to diverge from that of England from the days of the first settlers. The two types of modern English, American and British, are thus 'related' in that they developed from a common source or 'parent', viz. 17th century English of England.

The Romance group of languages in Europe provides a clear example of this process at work in the case of distinct languages. The spoken Latin of 2,000 years ago evolved into the various modern Romance languages (principally Italian, French, Spanish, Portuguese and Romanian) - due to a number of factors, such as the geographical separation of the various communities of Latin speakers throughout the Roman Empire, the lack of centralising influences once the empire had declined, and the different linguistic influences exercised by the various 'native' languages spoken in each of the provinces. Today's Romance languages are in most cases mutually incomprehensible, though they do have a great deal in common in terms of their grammatical structure, their vocabulary and their sound systems. Such common ground between the languages, which could not possibly be the result of coincidence, is what would have suggested that they have evolved from a common source, i.e. are 'genetically' related, even if all traces of the Latin language had vanished from history. Fortunately, the evidence of a common 'parent' language for the Romance family, Latin, is intact. In the case of other European groups of languages, Celtic, Germanic and Slavonic, where similar family relationships have been established, there remain no records of an ancestral language.

1.2 The Indo-European language family

It was noticed by European scholars in the late 18th century that Sanskrit, the classical language of India, had much in common with Classical Greek and Latin, as well as with some other languages of Europe. In this way the idea of a superordinate, or three-generation, language family arose, to which the name 'Indo-European' has been given, comprising languages as geographically separated as the Germanic and Celtic families in the west, and the descendants of Sanskrit in the east (Figure 1).

FIGURE 1: THE MAIN BRANCHES OF THE INDO-EUROPEAN LANGUAGE FAMILY

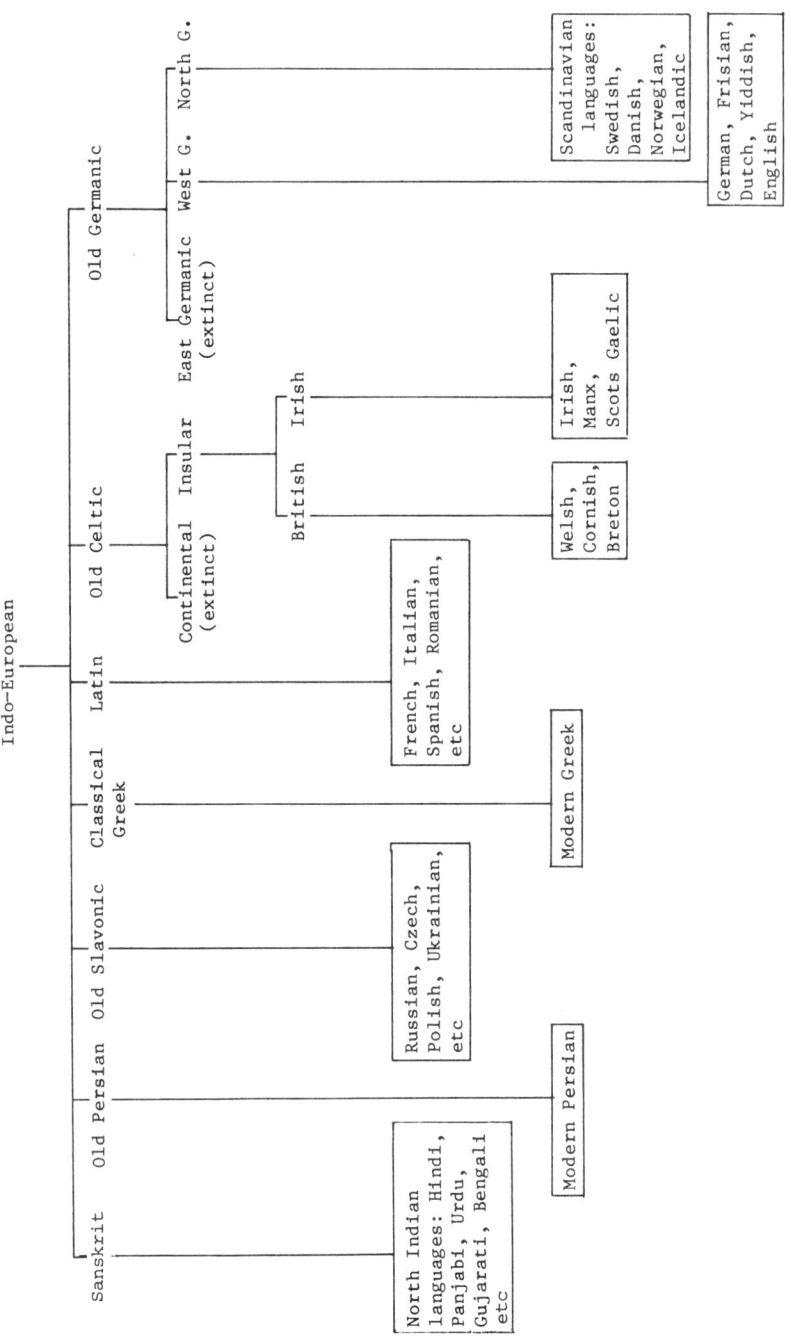

The descendants of Sanskrit comprise the major modern languages of the northern part of the Indian Subcontinent, and include all those with which this book is principally concerned – Panjabi, Gujarati, Bengali, Urdu and Hindi. This language family, the Indo-Aryan, is the subject of the next chapter.

Clearly, the common ground between the modern languages of the superordinate family is much harder to perceive than that which links members of each of the constituent families: thus French and Italian can be said to have a 'sister' relationship within the Romance family, sharing a common 'parent', whereas French and Panjabi have a common 'grandparent' in the Indo-European extended family and are more like cousins. (Of course, no written evidence exists for the Indo-European 'grandparent' language.) However, the modern languages of the extended family do have a number of characteristics and features in common, which will be illustrated here by some of the correspondences occurring between the sound systems of various languages:

1. A large number of words which begin with the sound p in Hindi (taking this language as representative of the Indo-Aryan branch of Indo-European) correspond to words of the same or similar meaning in English (representative of the Germanic branch) which begin with the sound f:

e.g. pitā = father; p̃āv = foot

2. Similarly, Hindi t often corresponds to the English th when at the beginning of a word:

e.g. tīn = three; tū = thou

3. Hindi d corresponds to English t:

e.g. do = two; das = ten

These examples are stated in more detail in Appendix I, where Latin, French, Greek and Sanskrit equivalents are also given, together with some examples of grammatical similarities between Sanskrit and the classical languages of Europe.

It is correspondences such as these which strongly suggest the idea of a single common origin for Latin, Classical Greek, Sanskrit and their modern derivatives, also for the Germanic languages (including English) and several other groups of languages. Despite the total lack of direct evidence for it, the grandparent language is usually referred to by the name of Indo-European, as if it had existed as an actual language of a community: indeed, plausible attempts have been made to reconstruct it on the basis of features common to its descendants.

7

However, what is of interest in the present discussion is not the particular nature of the Indo-European language but rather the fact that there are regular, systematic correspondences occurring between the modern descendants of Sanskrit (Hindi etc) and the languages of Western Europe (English, French etc). Thus, the fact that the numerals two and three have the same initial sounds in French and Hindi ('deux', 'trois', and 'do', 'tīn' respectively) is not the result of chance, but is part of a broader pattern. Awareness of patterns such as this can make the task of learning the grammar and vocabulary of the modern Indo-Aryan languages much less daunting. A more important point has already been made in the Introduction, namely that the Indo-European language family relationship is a significant factor linking most of the South Asian linguistic minorities in Britain to the dominant English language majority population. This is worth remembering when it is a minority's differences which are so often emphasised.

2. South Asian languages - linguistic background and characteristics

2.1 Background

The five languages which form the focus of this book - Panjabi, Gujarati, Bengali, Urdu and Hindi - all belong to the Indo-Aryan branch of Indo-European. This branch also includes the following major languages: Marathi, Oriya and Assamese (spoken in India), Sindhi (India and Pakistan), Nepalese (Nepal) and Sinhalese (Sri Lanka). The Indo-Aryan languages as a whole are spoken by about three-quarters of the population of South Asia. (The remainder of the population speak non-Indo-European languages: these belong to the Dravidian, Austro-Asiatic and Sino-Tibetan language families, which are described briefly in Appendix II.)

The language which stands in the same relationship to the modern Indo-Aryan languages as does Latin to the modern Romance languages is Sanskrit, the classical language of India and in particular of the Hindu religion. The external relationship of Sanskrit to Latin, Classical Greek, etc was outlined in the previous chapter; here, we will consider the evolution, internal to South Asia, of Sanskrit into its modern descendants.

It is impossible to establish with certainty when Sanskrit was in use as a living language. The earliest surviving inscriptions found in India are the edicts of the Emperor Ashoka (3rd century B.C.), inscribed on rocks and pillars. These are in Prakrit, a group of dialects which represent a later stage of linguistic evolution than Sanskrit. This implies that by the 3rd century B.C. Classical Sanskrit was no longer a spoken vernacular. The earliest known compositions (as opposed to written records) in Sanskrit are the Vedic Hymns (Rigveda etc), which are generally reckoned to date from the period when the earliest Indo-Aryan speaking peoples were migrating into the Indian Subcontinent from the North-West, i.e. about 1500 B.C.. The Vedic hymns were handed down orally from generation to generation for centuries, and because of their sacred character not a syllable was changed. (Were it not for this extraordinarily strict oral tradition, we would have no knowledge today of the Vedas and the other early literature associated with them, because in ancient India there was no manuscript material durable enough to withstand the climatic conditions.) Thus the old Indo-Aryan language, which was known as 'Sanskrit' (meaning 'polished'), became codified or 'frozen' at a stage of development slightly later than that of the Vedic hymns. It was preserved in that form as a learned language for scholarship and religion, with a role not unlike that of Latin in Medieval Europe.

This use of the language for written and scholarly purposes

continued until about the 10th century A.D., when composition in Sanskrit began to give way to writing in the local vernaculars. By then a prodigious amount of literature had been produced in Sanskrit: prose, poetry and drama, works both secular and sacred, and 'non-literary' writing in every conceivable branch of scholarship. Throughout the centuries the form of the language remained completely unchanged. Today Sanskrit continues to be used for certain ritual purposes in Hinduism, sacred texts such as the Bhagavad Gita being read in Sanskrit, and even the conversational use of Sanskrit is practised by some Hindu priests.

In the meantime, while Sanskrit was being used in its immutable form down the centuries, the spoken Indo-Aryan vernaculars in different parts of the north of India had diverged gradually, and by the Prakrit stage clear regional differences had appeared. (The word 'Prakrit' meant 'natural, ordinary', i.e. not 'pure' like Sanskrit.) The Prakrit dialects themselves had a certain amount of literary use from about the 6th century B.C. onwards, in addition to being used for official inscriptions (e.g. those of Ashoka, mentioned above), but they were always subordinate in status to Sanskrit. (One exception to this was Pali, the particular Prakrit dialect which became the vehicle for the religious literature of the Theravada branch of Buddhism, and which thrives today as the classical and liturgical language of Sri Lankan and South-East Asian Buddhists.)

2.2 Characteristics

By about the year 1000 A.D. the earliest forms of the modern Indo-Aryan languages had begun to emerge, showing marked differences from the structure of Sanskrit. For example, whereas Sanskrit, like Latin and Greek, had used special endings on words to show their function in a sentence (for subject, object, etc in nouns; person and tense in verbs), the modern Indo-Aryan languages, like their modern Romance cousins, had become more 'analytic' in character, relying on the order of words and other grammatical processes, rather than on word endings, to indicate these functions. This development was greatly assisted by phonetic changes in the spoken language, which resulted in the gradual disappearance of the grammatically important word endings of Sanskrit, just as happened in the transition from Latin to French.

An additional factor helping to determine the character of the modern languages which evolved from Sanskrit was the nature of the languages spoken in the Subcontinent by the population settled there before the advent of the Indo-Aryan speaking people. As mentioned above, these languages are not Indo-European but belong to other linguistic family classifications, such as Dravidian. The influence exercised by these languages on the development of Indo-Aryan might have occurred in the following manner: as the Indo-Aryan speaking invaders became dominant in the northern parts of the Subcontinent, sometime during the second millennium B.C., the conquered population would have learned the language of their new masters, but imperfectly, carrying over features of their mother tongue into the newly-acquired language. (This is a universal aspect of language learning, which may be observed in language classrooms everywhere!) The subject population was in fact much more numerous than the dominant group, and as the new language was passed on to the following generations as their mother tongue, such borrowed features gradually became the norm and ceased to be regarded as 'foreigners' mistakes'.

An example of Dravidian influence on modern Indo-Aryan is thought to be the use of 'postpositions', which correspond to prepositions in other modern Indo-European languages, such as the Romance and Germanic language groups. Whereas the general tendency in the evolution of Indo-European languages was for prepositions (i.e. words which precede, are pre-posed to, nouns or noun phrases) to do part of the grammatical work of the older word endings, the Indo-Aryan languages are unique in having developed post-positions (which follow nouns) to play the same role. This is almost certainly the result of the influence of Dravidian mother tongues, which themselves use postpositions.

Processes such as this can result in what is known as linguistic 'convergence', whereby neighbouring languages, which are not necessarily related historically and which may have been quite dissimilar originally, become more like each other. Such processes occurred in both directions in the Indian Subcontinent: not only were the Indo-Aryan languages influenced by the languages of the earlier population, but Indo-Aryan itself has influenced the surviving languages of the Dravidian and other families. Linguistic convergence is hastened by the widespread incidence of bi- and multi-lingualism amongst the population concerned, which seems to have long been a characteristic of the Subcontinent. As a result, languages in South Asia share many specifically 'Indian' features, and the region is recognised as a classic example of the notion of a 'linguistic area' (where totally unrelated languages exhibit several features in common). The implication for outsiders coming to grips with South Asian languages is that beneath the bewildering diversity there are many unifying strands.

A few characterics which are common to these languages, and which differentiate them from English, will now be presented, under the headings of grammar, sounds, scripts and vocabulary. The characteristic features of grammar and sounds presented below, which are completely different from English and other Indo-European languages, are invariably due to the influence of the non-Indo-European languages of South Asia.

: Grammatical examples are taken from Hindi, representing the Indo-Aryan languages as a whole, and are accompanied by both word-for-word and natural English translations. The spelling used here to transcribe Hindi should be easy to follow. Notations which might not be readily apparent are: i) the tilde ($\sim$), which indicates that the vowel over which it is placed is nasalised; and ii) the underlining of a consonant (e.g. <u>t</u>), which indicates a manner of pronunciation with the tip of the tongue pulled back to the roof of the mouth. (These are called retroflex consonants; they are discussed under <u>sounds</u> below.)

I. GRAMMAR

Word order

i) The basic order of words in sentences is Subject-Object-Verb (SOV), which contrasts with Subject-Verb-Object (SVO) word order of English and many other Western languages.

      e.g. mohan hindī boltā-hai
          Mohan Hindi speaks

      Mohan speaks Hindi.

ii) Postpositions are used instead of prepositions, as already mentioned:

      e.g. vah landan mẽ rahtā-hai
          he London in lives

      He lives in London.

(A few English compound words show a similar construction, e.g. hereafter (meaning: after 'here', after this time), therein, etc.)

Articles

Indo-Aryan languages have neither definite (the) nor indefinite (a, an) articles.

      e.g. la<u>r</u>kā seb   khā-rahā thā
          boy   apple eating   was

      A (or The) boy was eating an (or the) apple.

The appropriate English translation will of course depend on the context.

Gender of nouns

In Panjabi, Urdu and Hindi there are two grammatical genders, masculine and feminine (as in French: 'le garçon(m) and 'la fille(f)). Gujarati additionally has a neuter gender, as in German. In Bengali on the other hand, gender is 'natural' rather than grammatical, with masculine gender corresponding to maleness etc, as in English. Grammatical 'agreement' (i.e. matching the shape of the endings of certain words) is very important, and it applies to both gender and number (singular vs. plural; again this is similar to the French 'le grand garçon, les grandes filles'). Adjectives agree with their nouns; and participles, which are important elements of verb constructions, agree with the subject of the sentence. Here are three different agreement forms for an adjective:-

e.g. barā larkā   bare larke   barī larkī
     big boy   big boys   big girl

Pronouns of address

As in most European languages (apart from modern standard English), there are at least two forms of the second person pronoun ('you'), for familiar and polite usage. The form of the verb changes according to the pronoun chosen.

e.g.   <u>polite</u>   <u>familiar</u>

     āp kahā̃ rahte—hai?   tum kahā̃ rahte—ho?
     you where live?   you where live?

     where do you live?   where do you live?

Verbs

i) The verb in a sentence usually consists of a phrase with two or more elements, rather than of a single word. It is very common to find an auxiliary verb in combination with a participle, as in the English construction consisting of the verb 'to be' with the present participle ('-ing') of another verb (as in 'she is reading'). In Indo-Aryan languages the auxiliary verb occupies the final position in the verb phrase, and therefore in the whole sentence.

e.g. a) ma͠i jātā hū̃
      I   going am

     I go (habitually)

b) ma͂i jā rahā   hū͂
   I   go 'continuing' am

   I am going (at the present moment)

ii) Further aspects of the grammar of verbs are given in Appendix
III.

II SOUNDS

Retroflex consonants

Indo-Aryan languages have two quite distinct kinds of 't' and 'd'
sounds. One is known in phonetic terms as dental, e.g. t (without
underlining): this is pronounced in the French rather than in the
English manner, i.e. with the tip of the tongue touching the upper
teeth rather than the upper gum. The other is described phonetically
as 'retroflex', e.g. t̲ (underlined): here the tongue tip is arched
back to make contact with the roof of the mouth. (Retroflex pronunciations of t and d contribute to the characteristic accent of
Indian English.) Several pairs of words are distinguished merely by
these different pronunciations, i.e. dental as opposed to retroflex.

        e.g. t̲op (= hat) vs. top (= cannon)

Aspiration of consonants

In English, many pairs of consonant sounds are distinguished by the
presence or absence of voicing, e.g. p (unvoiced) vs. b (voiced), k
vs. g, t vs. d, etc. The corresponding Indo-Aryan sounds are
distinguished not only on the dimension of voicing, but also on a
further dimension of aspiration. Thus, besides the unvoiced - voiced
pair of sounds p vs. b, which are unaspirated, there is also an
aspirated pair of unvoiced and voiced sounds, ph vs. bh.

Aspiration involves a slight puff of air released as the consonant
is articulated. In fact, the usual English pronunciation of p,
especially at the beginning of a word, is an aspirated variety. For
this reason, Indo-Aryan unaspirated p comes over to the English ear
like b; it is the Indo-Aryan aspirated ph which most closely resembles English p.

The voiced aspirates (bh, etc) of Indo-Aryan languages have no
counterparts in western languages, except over syllable boundaries
in compound words such as madhouse (-dh-). (Panjabi forms an excep-

14

tion on this point, in that it has no voiced aspirated sounds as such. This will be mentioned again in the section (3.1) devoted specifically to Panjabi.)

Here is a table of the complete system of Indo–Aryan consonants to which these two distinctions (voicing and aspiration) apply:

place of articulation	voiceless		voiced	
	unaspirated	aspirated	unaspirated	aspirated
rear palate	k	kh	g	gh
mid palate	c	ch	j	jh
tongue tip (retroflex*)	t̲	t̲h	d̲	d̲h
tongue tip (dental*)	t	th	d	dh
lips	p	ph	b	bh

(* see above on retroflex consonants)

III SCRIPTS

Apart from the Perso–Arabic script used for Urdu, all the modern South Asian scripts are derived from that used in the Ashokan inscriptions of the 3rd century B.C. (mentioned in 2.1) which is itself thought to be ultimately of Semitic origin. The most widely used South Asian script is Devanagari. This is used for writing Hindi and certain other languages, and it is the script in which Sanskrit is generally written and printed today. The Panjabi script (called Gurmukhi) and the Gujarati and Bengali scripts are closely related to Devanagari. Due to this family relationship, all these scripts have certain characteristics in common (some of which are outlined below), although they are as different in external appearance as the Roman, Greek and Cyrillic (Russian) alphabets of Europe, which are also related to each other through a common ancestor (the Phoenician script).

Technically speaking, the Indian scripts are not so much alphabets as syllabaries. That is to say that a consonant 'letter' alone can represent a complete syllable, consisting of the consonant itself followed by the short vowel a; e.g. the syllables pa, ta, ka are represented by the letters p, t, k alone. Where a syllable consists of a consonant followed by any vowel other than short a, e.g. pā, pi, pe, etc, these other vowel sounds are indicated by signs placed above, below, after or before the consonant letter. There are also separate letters representing the vowels when they are not linked to a preceding consonant, i.e. when they stand alone or at the beginning of a word.

Where one consonant is followed immediately by another, without any intervening vowel (e.g. prāpta, rather than parāpata), the two adjacent consonants are normally combined in the script, with one or both being represented in a reduced or modified form. In the example given the two consonant sequences pr and pt are represented by such 'conjunct' consonant letters. Compared with the 35 simple consonant letters of the Devangari script, there are about 150 conjunct letters, or digraphs. In most, but not all, of these, the constituent consonants are easily recognisable in reading, though in writing more effort is needed by the learner to produce the conjuncts appropriately.

The general appearance of many of the South Asian scripts is that of letters seeming to hang from a line, compared with western scripts which are written above a line, whether ruled or imaginary. This 'line' of the South Asian scripts is actually a component part of most of the letters and is drawn as the writing proceeds. All these scripts are written horizontally, from left to right, and none of them have separate capital letters. (Urdu is of course written from right to left, as are Persian and Arabic with which it shares its scripts.)

Figure 2: Samples of South Asian scripts commonly used in Britain

English	Islamabad	Delhi	Dacca
Characteristic pronunciation in South Asia:	islāmābād	dillī	ḏhākā
Panjabi (Gurmukhi):	ਇਿਸਲਾਮਾਬਾਦ	ਦਿੱਲੀ	ਢਾਕਾ
Gujarati:	ઇસ્લામાબાદ	દિલ્લી	ઢાકા
Bengali:	ইসলামাবাদ	দিল্লী	ঢাকা
Hindi (Devanagari):	इस्लामाबाद	दिल्ली	ढाका
Urdu (Perso-Arabic):	اسلام آباد	دہلی	ڈھاکا

16

IV VOCABULARY

The reason for including vocabulary in this series of distinctive characteristics of Indo-Aryan languages is the strong association between vocabulary items and the religious affiliation of speakers or writers. Within a given Indo-Aryan language, certain items of vocabulary are far more likely to be used by members of one particular religious grouping, while other items, equivalent in meaning, will be used by another such grouping. Moreover, as will be described in the following chapter, it is the association of religious background with vocabulary choice (coupled with the use of two separate scripts) which has led to Hindi and Urdu being recognised as separate languages, when on narrowly linguistic grounds they might reasonably be supposed to be variants of one and the same language. This influence of different religious affiliations on aspects of language use has no counterpart in Europe.

Fortunately for learners of South Asian languages, the vast majority of the lexical items of each language are quite neutral as to religious association. Most words in the modern Indo-Aryan languages derive from the oldest stage of Indo-Aryan, known to us in the form of Sanskrit, whence they have evolved to take their various modern shapes in the different languages. For example, Hindi and Urdu aj and Panjabi aj (today) derive from Sanskrit adya; Hindi and Urdu ãkh and Panjabi akkh (eye) are from Sanskrit akshi. Additionally, a relatively small number of words originating from non-Indo-Aryan languages (the Dravidian languages, etc) have been naturalised in Indo-Aryan, in some cases since the period of Sanskrit itself; they form part of the native Indian stock of vocabulary.

However, South Asia has been subject to invasion and foreign rule, especially during the last thousand years. In this respect the region is of course far from unique. A natural result of political domination by outsiders speaking other languages has been the absorption of large numbers of words from the languages of the rulers into the 'native' languages. In this way, vocabulary has entered the Indo-Aryan languages from Turkish, Arabic, Persian and English. Often, a 'foreign' word has been borrowed because no suitable native word exists for a concept, as in the case of Arabic and Persian words being used for Islamic concepts, and English words for Western concepts and artefacts. In many cases, however, a foreign word would displace a perfectly good native word, for social rather than linguistic reasons. (To see similar processes at work in the historical evolution of English, consider the Scandinavian and French elements in our vocabulary, which are to some extent the direct results of the Danish and Norman conquests.)

The 'religious' aspect of vocabulary choice, which distinguishes the South Asian language situation, has arisen from the ready availability, and high prestige, of Arabic and Persian models of language for Muslims, and the corresponding attraction of Sanskrit for Hindus. Thus, whereas certain Muslims would tend to lard their speech and writing with Persian and Arabic words and phrases, determined Hindus would attempt to counter the Islamicisation of their language by the use of classical Sanskrit vocabulary. The type of language most likely to be affected by wholesale importation of this sort, from whichever source, is serious writing or discussion on topics such as religion itself, culture, philosophy, law - indeed anything that goes beyond the concrete, everyday uses of language.

In effect, words can be 'put on' like styles of dress - liberal use of Persian and Arabic words marks a person out as a Muslim, an admirer of the Persian culture and life-style of the Muslim rulers; similar use of Sanskritisms indicates a Hindu, a defender of things Indian against the 'foreign' ways of the rulers. The results are two distinct styles, Hindu and Muslim, of a particular language, such as Gujarati. It cannot be repeated too often, however, that what is common to the two styles, and what is of greatest importance to a learner of the language, far outweighs the number of specific elements which are peculiar to a particular style.

3. South Asian languages - socio-historical background and present-day status

The major South Asian languages spoken in Britain are (in decreasing order of numbers of native speakers): Panjabi, Gujarati, Bengali, Urdu and Hindi, which all belong to the Indo-Aryan language family, described in the previous chapter. These have been identified as the 'major' languages in this country, and thus selected for prominent discussion in this book, as they are the South Asian languages which feature most prominently in surveys of Britain's minority languages. (For references to such surveys see Note 1 on p 46.) They are the South Asian languages chosen by the BBC for use in publicity and support materials for its 'Speak For Yourself' series, and by various other publicity undertakings, such as the Stop Rickets Campaign. However, besides these there are several other South Asian languages which have smaller communities of speakers settled in Britain, such as Marathi (Indo-Aryan), Tamil and Telugu (both Dravidian). Many speakers of these languages will also have a working knowledge of one of the languages listed above, espcially of Urdu or Hindi.

This chapter will discuss briefly each of these five major languages. They will be described not in linguistic terms, but from a social and cultural point of view, that is in terms of the historical background of the communities who use them in the Indian Subcontinent, and in terms of the people settled in Britain who speak each language. (A short list of published materials for learning these languages is given in Appendix IV).

Firstly, however, a note of caution must be sounded about the statistics given in what follows, relating to numbers of speakers of particular languages. This is because accurate figures are very difficult to obtain, both in respect of the South Asian countries, and in respect of the linguistic minorities in Britain. The latest generally available figures for the total population of the Subcontinent are from the 1971 national censuses, which give a combined population for Pakistan, India and (what is now) Bangladesh of 692 million. Tentative figures for speakers of individual languages will be given in the appropriate sections below, though it should be pointed out that the census data is not entirely reliable on the subject of language. For example, there are particular difficulties associated with the enumeration of speakers of Urdu and Hindi: these too will be outlined below.

The numbers of speakers of particular South Asian languages in Britain can also be no more than reasoned estimates, due to the lack of any question on linguistic or ethnic affiliations in UK censuses (Celtic areas apart). In the 1971 census, some data was recorded on the overseas-born population, but this relates merely to country of origin with no linguistic distinctions (see Note 2 on p 46). The figures given below relating to speakers of the major South Asian languages in Britain were based on an estimate of an overall UK population of South Asian origin or parentage totalling more than 1 million in 1981. This estimate, and its breakdown into particular languages, was made informally by a member of the former Linguistic Minorities Project, and is not intended to provide any more than a very approximate indication of the South Asian contribution to linguistic diversity in Britain. (For readers interested in the problems of language survey and census work in the context of linguistic minorities in Britain, useful references are given in Note 3 on p 46.)

3.1 Panjabi

(Note: there are two major categories of Panjabi speakers in Britain, classified according to country of origin, together with religious affiliations and script usage. For this reason, the background to the distinctions among Panjabi speakers will be described in some detail.)

Panjabi is the state language of the Indian State of Panjab, and in its various dialects is spoken by about 37 million people throughout the geographical Panjab, which extends over some other administrative divisions within India besides Panjab State, and over a large part of Pakistan.

There are two major dialect groups: (i) Eastern Panjabi, which includes Standard Panjabi, based on the area between Amritsar (India) and Lahore (Pakistan); ii) Western Panjabi, spoken entirely within Pakistan. The Eastern Panjabi dialects are in many respects very similar to Hindi and Urdu.

Literary use

Panjabi has long been used for the writing of mystical and religious verse, also of folk ballads and romances; the earliest such works date from the 13th century. The main impetus to the development of the language for literary and religious purposes (and indeed to the development of Panjabi nationalism) came from the Sikh religion, founded by Guru Nanak (1469-1539). (However, it is characteristic of the polyglot nature of South Asian life that the bulk of the early Sikh scriptures are not composed exclusively in Panjabi but also include a variety of Hindi dialects.) In the 20th century the language has been the vehicle for a considerable output of secular verse and prose.

Background to the religious distinctions

The terms 'Sikh' and 'Panjabi' are often taken to be synonymous. However, while it is rare in practice to find a Sikh who is not Panjabi by language and provenance, the inhabitants of the geographical Panjab region belong to three main cultural-religious groupings: Hinduism, Islam and Sikhism. Further, any outline of the status of Panjabi as a language must take into account not only religious factors but also the political cleavage of the region by the Indo-Pakistan border at Independence.

The Panjab was under Muslim rule from the 11th to about the mid 18th centry. During this period, Islam and Hinduism co-existed, sometimes peacefully, sometimes antagonistically, depending on the inclination of the ruler of the time. (For example, the Mughal Emperor Akbar was an advocate of reconciliation.) Several attempts were made at bringing together these two religions; the best known 'offspring' of the two is Sikhism, which originally incorporated the mystic and devotional elements of both Hinduism and Islam.

As Muslim power declined, as elsewhere in India, in the 18th century, Sikhs gradually gained control of the administration of the Panjab, and a Sikh state existed for nearly a century until the British takeover of the region in 1849. On Indian Independence in 1947, the province was divided between Pakistan and India, according to the prevailing religious majority, i.e. Muslims to the North and West, Sikhs and Hindus to the South and East. There were large minority populations on each side, who had little option but to uproot and migrate across the new frontier. That migration was accompanied by much communal hatred and violence, memories of which have been kept alive by the continuing political disputes between India and Pakistan and the resulting border conflicts of 1965 and 1971.

Present role of Panjabi in Pakistan and India

On the Pakistan side, the Panjab formed part of the West Province of the former 'two-wing' Pakistan, but since 1970 it has been a province in its own right (capital: Lahore). The Panjabi language, however, has never had a generally recognised status in Pakistan: it is Urdu, the national language, which is used at all levels in the educational process, as well as for religious purposes. Thus, literacy in Pakistan means the ability to read and write Urdu, a second language for most of the population of Pakistan. The language of the home and of informal conversation throughout the Panjab region, and in parts of Pakistan-administered Kashmir, is Panjabi in its various dialects. In higher-status activities such as administration, law, education, religion, etc Urdu is used; it is also used in all spheres, including the domestic, for any activity involving writing (correspondence, accounts, memos, etc).

On the Indian side, the original Panjab state which was constituted after Independence contained both a Sikh and a Hindu population. Those were both largely Panjabi-speaking, but whereas for the Sikhs the Panjabi language itself was the valued language of literacy and high culture, for the Hindu community the valued language in this sense was Hindi. In 1966 the southern portion of the state, with a majority Hindu population, was separated off to form the new state of Haryana, with Hindi as the official language. This move followed India's previous practice of basing political states on major language areas. The capital city of both states is Chandigarh.

Even in the present Indian Panjab State, of which the official language is of course Panjabi, Sikhs represent only 60% of the population, the remainder being largely Hindu. Sikhs themselves have migrated widely over India, South-East Asia and other parts of the world, including Britain.

Religious differences in scripts and vocabulary

The use of Panjabi by the three distinct religious communities – Muslim, Hindu and Sikh – has led to the language being associated with three different scripts – the Perso-Arabic, Devanagari and Gurmukhi respectively.

i) Perso-Arabic: actually, Panjabi is only rarely written in this script, as this practice has little or no official standing in Pakistan. (One exception to this generalisation is the teaching of Panjabi language and literature at universities in Pakistan, which involves the study of Panjabi texts in the Perso-Arabic script.) The main reason for discussing this script in connection with the Panjabi language is that for Panjabi-speaking Pakistanis this is their main method of writing, although as stated earlier, the language which is written is not Panjabi but Urdu.

ii) Devanagari: Hindi language in the Devanagari script is the usual mode of writing for Panjabi-speaking Hindus. Devanagari is also the normal script used for Sanskrit.

iii) Sikhs write Panjabi in the Gurmukhi script. From its appearance, this script might be a naturally evolved relative of the Devanagari script; actually, it is believed to have been invented in the 16th century specifically for the writing of the Sikh scriptures. Gurmukhi is regarded by Sikhs as the only proper script for the Panjabi language. The official written medium in Panjab State (India) is Panjabi language in the Gurmukhi script.

In addition to the question of script usage which differentiates the religious communities, there are the usual South Asian vocabulary distinctions (see section 2.2.IV, p 17). Muslims draw on Persian and

Arabic words to fill the gaps where native Panjabi vocabulary is inadequate, and Hindus and Sikhs do likewise with both Hindi and Sanskrit words.

A note on the sound system of Panjabi

One important way in which Panjabi differs from Hindi, Urdu and the other Indo-Aryan languages is that it has no voiced aspirate sounds (see section 2.2.II, p 14). The sounds of Panjabi which correspond to the voiced aspirates (e.g. bh) of the other languages are voiceless unaspirated consonants (e.g. p) which are accompanied by a 'low tone' pronunciation in the syllable in which they occur. In this way Panjabi is to some extent a 'tonal language', like Chinese: given the same sequence of sounds in a syllable, a change in the tone (or pitch level) on which the syllable is pronounced can effect a change in the meaning. Examples: kor̲ā (level tone on first syllable = whip, corresponding to Hindi and Urdu kor̲ā); but kor̲ā (low tone on first syllable = horse, corresponding to Hindi and Urdu ghor̲ā).

Panjabi-speakers in Britain

Panjabi speakers in Britain, no less than in South Asia, may be categorised according to what part of the Panjab region they originate from, together with what dialect they speak, what scripts they are familiar with and their religious adherence. The two main categories of Panjabi-speakers in Britain are:

i) Sikhs, who formed the first large category of South Asian migrants to Britain, settlement commencing in the early post-war years. They total upwards of 400,000, with a major settlement centred on Southall in the London Borough of Ealing, and substantial communities also in Coventry, Birmingham, the London Borough of Newham, and in certain smaller towns, such as Gravesend. Their written language is Panjabi in the Gurmukhi script; those who were educated in pre-Independence India may have Urdu (Perso-Arabic script) as a second language, while those who were educated in India after Independence are likely to have Hindi (Devanagari script) as a second language.

There are many older Sikhs with skills in all three writing systems.

ii) Muslims, totalling perhaps 200,000, with large concentrations in cities in West Yorkshire, e.g. Bradford, also in Lancashire and Greater Manchester, Birmingham and parts of London. They originate from Pakistan proper and what is known as Azad Kashmir, i.e. that part of the disputed State of Jammu and Kashmir which is administered by Pakistan. Many of those who came to Britain from Azad

23

Kashmir originate from the Mirpur district, and speak the Mirpuri dialect of Panjabi. The language of literacy and the second spoken language for all Panjabi-speaking Muslims in Britain is of course Urdu.

Inasmuch as Hindi and Urdu are, from a linguistic point of view, the same language in spoken form, these two categories of Panjabi speakers in Britain may be said to share both a common first language (i.e. Panjabi in its various dialects) and a common second language (i.e. Hindi-Urdu). It is the question of script and, more importantly, the different literary-cultural-religious traditions which divide them.

3.2 Gujarati

Gujarati is the state language of Gujarat in western India, spoken by approximately 25 million people.

Literary use

There are fragments of literature dating from the 12th century which are claimed as Gujarati, though some of this early writing is hard to distinguish linguistically from neighbouring Rajasthani. Gujarati came into its own as an independent literary medium in the 14th century, and the use of the language for modern, western-influenced literature developed in the mid 19th century. Its status was greatly boosted by Gandhi (1869-1948), a native of Gujarat, who advocated the use of regional vernaculars such as Gujarati for local administration in place of a pan-Indian language such as English or Urdu.

Background to religious distinctions

Like much of North India, the Gujarat area came under Muslim rule around 1300 A.D. and remained so until the Hindu Marathas took control in the middle of the 18th century. The Marathas in their turn were displaced by the British early in the 19th century, and at the time of Independence the Gujarat region was a part of Bombay State. In 1960 this state was split on linguistic lines into its two major components: Gujarat State to the north (capital: until 1970 – Ahmedabad, since then – Gandhinagar), and Maharashtra State to the south (capital: Bombay); the state language of the latter is Marathi, but there is a very large community of Gujarati speakers in Bombay City.

This history is reflected in the vocabulary of Gujarati. The Muslims introduced a large number of Persian and Arabic words, which are specially prominent in the language of Gujarati Muslims. In the

Maratha period, a substantial number of words were absorbed from the Marathi language. Besides English, another Western source of vocabulary was Portuguese, through Portugal's coastal settlements in western India dating from the 16th century.

An important linguistic minority in Gujarat are the Kutchi speakers, from the coastal region called Kutch which lies between Gujarat and Sind (Pakistan). Their language (Kutchi) is regarded by linguists as a variety of Sindhi, but as it has so many similarities with Gujarati it is commonly considered to be a dialect of the latter. Those Hindu Kutchi speakers who found themselves on the Pakistan side of the border at Partition fled to Gujarat, on the Indian side.

Gujarati-speakers in Britain

The location on the western seaboard of India and the early contact with the Portuguese has meant that Gujarat has tended to be outward-looking, and indeed its people, like the Sikhs, have a long tradition of emigrating, especially to Southern and East Africa. Gujarati speakers in Britain, who include Kutchi speakers, have come either directly from India or via East Africa. They are settled in various cities, with a large concentration of Hindus in Leicester and in the London Borough of Brent, and of Muslims in Batley in West Yorkshire. Their total is estimated at 300,000.

One linguistic distinction between Hindu and Muslim speakers of Gujarati in Britain, apart from vocabulary differences, is that while both communities use the Gujarati language for most purposes and write it in the same Indian script, the Hindus use Gujarati itself for religious purposes, and the Muslims Urdu (and Arabic). Muslim children are encouraged to learn to read and write Urdu; indeed, many Muslim Gujarati speakers feel that Urdu will thrive for much longer than Gujarati as their community language in the British context.

3.3 Bengali

Bengali is the national language of Bangladesh – the land ('desh') of Bengalis. It is also the state language of West Bengal (India), and is widely spoken in the neighbouring Indian states of Assam, Bihar, Orissa and Tripura, as well as in adjacent parts of Burma. In its various dialects it is spoken by more than 140 million people. By its speakers, the language is known as 'Bangla'.

Literary use

The oldest evidence of a distinct Bengali language is some Old

Bengali verse dating from about 1000 A.D. The history of the modern language goes back to the beginning of the 19th century, when Bengali writing began to respond to Western literary influences - it was in fact the first among Indian literatures to do so. The Bengali language has developed into the medium of one of the world's great literatures, with a vast accumulation of writings in prose, poetry and drama. The work of the Bengali poet Rabindranath Tagore (1861-1941) is of international renown.

Background to religious distinctions

As a result of Muslim rule in India there has been a strong Persian influence in Bengal (as in all parts of North India) since the 13th century; indeed, the language of the law courts was Persian, even in the early phases of British rule in the province, until the English language took over this role in 1836. Since the 18th century Persian, Arabic and Turkish words have entered Bengali in large numbers, especially in the literary and religious writings of Muslims. Attempts were made by Muslims to popularise the writing of Bengali in the Persian script, but these were not successful. Standard Bengali is thus a unified language, using a single Indian script, with some lexical differentiation between the two religious communities for the expression of religious and cultural concepts.

The two communities - Hindu and Muslim - were to some extent geographically distinct in the pre-Independence province of Bengal, with Hindus in the west and Muslims in the east. At Partition the province was split along religious lines (with the inevitable minorities on each side who became refugees), resulting in the formation of the Indian West Bengal State (capital: Calcutta) and the former East Wing of Pakistan, which in 1971 became Bangladesh (capital: Dacca).

Bengali speakers in Britain

Most Bengali speakers settled in Britain (estimated total 100,000) originate from Bangladesh (or former East Pakistan) and are Muslims by religion. They are concentrated mainly in the East End of London, particularly Spitalfields and Shadwell in the London Borough of Tower Hamlets, with further major settlements in Manchester, Birmingham, Bradford and other cities in England and Scotland.

Although it is hard to find exact figures, it is clear from survey reports that a large proportion of Bengali speakers in Britain are from Sylhet District in the north-east of Bangladesh, where the vernacular (Sylheti) differs considerably from Standard Bengali. When asked about their mother tongue, many Sylheti speakers in Britain tend to identify themselves as 'Bengali' speakers, implying the standard language, even if their everyday speech is Sylheti.

3.4 Urdu and 3.5 Hindi

(Note: Urdu and Hindi are considered by linguists to be two styles of a single language, differing in script and in some aspects of vocabulary. They will therefore be treated together. Although they are not widely spoken mother tongues of South Asians in Britain, the historical background to Urdu and Hindi will be described in some detail because of the importance of these languages both in South Asia and for people in Britain with South Asian connections.)

Urdu is the national language of Pakistan. In India it has the status of one of the fifteen languages recognised by the constitution though, unlike most of the other recognised languages, it is not connected specifically with any particular state. Hindi is the national language of India as a whole, and is also the state language of Uttar Pradesh, Haryana, Rajasthan, Madhya Pradesh and Bihar. Numbers of speakers for Urdu and Hindi will be discussed below, together with the difficulties involved in the interpretation of the census statistics.

The origins of the two language names are as follows:

'Urdu' is an abbreviated form of a Persian expression, 'zaban-e-urdu', meaning 'language of the (military) camp', which is itself a shortening of 'zaban-e-urdu-e-mu'alla' (language of the exalted (i.e. imperial) camp).

The name 'Hindi' is also Persian in origin; it is an adjective meaning 'Indian'. The Persian words 'Hind' and 'Hindostan' both mean 'India', and are ultimately derived from the ancient Indian designation for the river Indus, 'Sindhu', by means of the replacement of initial s by h, which is a regular feature of Persian. (The English name of the country 'India' has of course the same origin, coming to us via the Greeks and the Romans with the loss of the initial letter. These names of the country therefore relate originally to the 'land of the Indus', the north-west part of the Subcontinent which was known earliest to the western world.)

Background to the religious distinctions

The everyday speech of the population inhabiting the north-central region of the subcontinent, extending south-eastward from the Delhi area along the Gangetic plain down to the borders of West Bengal, forms a large group of dialects known collectively as the 'Hindi' dialects. These form a continuum, or chain, in which neighbouring dialects are very similar, while between the western and eastern extremes the differences are so great as to suggest separate languages rather than dialects.

Some of these dialects have a long tradition of literary use: early verse writing which is clearly in a variety of Hindi dates from the 14th century. During the 16th and 17th centuries a vast amount of Hindu devotional and epic poetry was produced in some of the dialects. (A major example of this is Tulsi Das's Eastern Hindi dialect version of the Classical Sanskrit epic of Rama, the Ramayana.) The literary and devotional use of these Hindi dialects continues to flourish today in various sects of Hinduism.

There was no reason inherent in Hinduism or in native Indian politics, why any particular one of these dialects should have become a standardised 'national' language, overwhelming all the others in prestige. That a particular Hindi dialect did become such a language resulted largely from the presence of 'foreign' rulers in north India. For a period of about 500 years, lasting until the middle of the 18th century, when British political influence began to be felt, large parts of the subcontinent were under Muslim rule, culminating in the reigns of the Mughal Emperors. The ruling Muslim dynasties were mostly of Turkish or Afghan origin, but their culture and way of life was based on that of Persia - their language, too, was Persian.

In the early centuries, none of the local Indian dialects or languages had any part to play in the Muslim pattern of administration. From about the 16th century, however, the dialect of the district just north of Delhi gradually acquired wider currency, being in close proximity to the Muslim court and being the speech of most of the native recruits in the army. While Persian remained the official language, this variety of Hindi spread all over India, through such channels as army encampments, bazaars and the administration networks. (Hence the Persian designation 'Urdu', i.e. 'camp' (language); another Persian name for the language was simply 'Hindostani', i.e. 'Indian', with its more familiar British spelling 'Hindustani'.) This language had no official status initially; it merely provided an informal link between the Persian-speaking rulers and the masses with their multiplicity of languages and dialects. (As a lingua franca it also formed a useful means of communication betwen Indians of different regions.)

An important step towards official recognition of the language occurred early in its development, still during the 16th century, when Urdu was cultivated as a literary language by Indian Muslims in the independent Muslim kingdoms of central India. (These were states which had broken free from the rule of the Muslim dynasties which were centred on north India.) The language as used in this way bore a strong Muslim stamp, using the Perso-Arabic script and taking most of its vocabulary from Persian, which itself had a large component of Arabic words.

However, Urdu was at base still an Indian language, though with an extensive Persian superstructure. This early literary use of the language therefore represented a blow against the cultural and linguistic domination of Persian itself, by setting a precedent for the use of a native Indian language or dialect, rather than Persian, in the composition of the emergent, largely Muslim, style of literature of the period. During the 18th century, the literary use of Urdu became widespread in the north, too. The next important step was for Urdu to replace Persian as the imperial language, which it did to some extent early in the British period. (For example, it was made the language of the lower courts and the revenue department in the North-West Provinces in 1837.)

There was an inevitable reaction in the 19th century by groups of Hindus, to whom this widely understood Muslim language must have seemed a threat. Their answer was to use the same local dialect which had provided the basis for Urdu, to write it in the Indian Devanagari script (also used for Sanskrit), and to take lexical items from Sanskrit where Urdu drew on Persian and Arabic. In this way, a wholly 'native' lingua franca, Hindu in character, was available as an alternative to Urdu. This 'new' language came to be called Hindi, or, to distinguish it from the group of Hindi dialects as a whole, High or Standard Hindi. By 1900 it was recognisd as a court language in the United Provinces.

Present role of Hindi and Urdu in India and Pakistan

As Hindi was already well-established in spoken form as a lingua franca throughout most of India (whether known as Urdu, Hindustani or Hindi), Standard Hindi became the inter-regional language of Hindus in most of north India during the late 19th and early 20th centuries, and when the Indian Constitution was framed in the early years of Independence it emerged as the national language for India. It also became the official language of states where the various Hindi dialects are current, such as Uttar Pradesh.

Urdu correspondingly became the national language of Pakistan, though it had no roots within the geographical confines of that country. Its roots are in the north-central regions of India, co-terminous with the Hindi language area, where many influential leaders of the Pakistan movement were based, in pre-Independence days. (Urdu never succeeded in establishing itself in the former East Pakistan, where Bengali was a unifying language for the population. By contrast, West Pakistan had a variety of native languages, notably Panjabi, Sindhi, Baluchi and Pashto; Urdu was thus more easily superimposed over these as a unifying national language.) In India, Urdu continues to function as the major second language for Muslims throughout the country.

Numbers of speakers of Urdu and Hindi

The figure reported for speakers of Urdu in the 1961 Indian census was 23 million, and for Hindi 123 million. Urdu speakers in Pakistan were reported as totalling 3 million, with a further 3 million claiming it as an 'additional language'. These figures must be interpreted cautiously, for the following reasons:

i) Many of the people enumerated in the Indian census as speaking Hindi will in fact be native speakers of some of the 'Hindi' dialects which may be sufficiently distant from the particular dialect on which Standard Hindi (and Urdu) is based, to constitute virtually separate languages from the latter. This applies especially to the Eastern Hindi dialects of areas such as Eastern Uttar Pradesh and Bihar. What will determine the extent to which such individuals will be able to understand or use Standard Hindi will be their level of education and their exposure to films or radio. Similar considerations apply to speakers of Urdu in the Indian censuses. In general terms it can be stated that up to the present neither Urdu nor Standard Hindi have been spoken natively in the subcontinent except by middle- and upper-class urban families. (This class restriction does not apply to the inhabitants of a relatively small region near Delhi, on whose dialect Urdu and Hindi were founded.)

ii) The very identity of the everyday spoken forms of Urdu and Standard Hindi make the distinction between the two for Indian census purposes of rather doubtful value.

iii) In fact, Hindi, Urdu (and Panjabi) census data is also fraught with other problems, largely political in origin (see Note 4, p 47).

Hindi and Urdu - same language or different?

The question of whether Hindi and Urdu are the 'same language' or not depends very much on the attitudes of their users, and totally opposing opinions are fiercely defended on this issue. A small-scale test was carried out recently among South Asians resident in Britain with the aim of finding out how unanimous users of Hindi and Urdu were in identifying particular words as belonging to either one or the other, or both, types of language. The results were somewhat unexpected (for reference see Note 5, p 47). Words of Persian and Arabic origin, which would normally be considered to be characteristic of Urdu, were identified by Hindus as 'Hindi'. On the other hand, words borrowed from Sanskrit (characteristic of a pure Hindi style), were identified by Muslims of Pakistani origin as 'Urdu'. The principle underlying these results seems to be: whatever is familiar is identified as belonging to one's own type of speech.

This investigation, while admittedly limited in scope, suggests that speakers are not necessarily aware of the origin of the words they use (Hindi and Urdu speakers might not be unique on this point!), and it seems to indicate that the boundary between the two styles is rather fluid. It certainly casts doubts on the more extreme claims that Urdu and Hindi are totally distinct languages.

Users of Urdu and Hindi in Britain

As far as the situation of Urdu and Hindi in Britain is concerned, while they do indeed figure prominently in the results of surveys of minority languages (see Note 1, p 46), the comments made above with reference to South Asia apply here, too. Thus it can be said that there are relatively few genuine native speakers of Urdu or standard Hindi settled in Britain, the exceptions being mainly among professional families. For this reason, no estimate of numbers of speakers in Britain will be suggested. The following paragraphs explain the significance of Urdu and Hindi for all communities of South Asian origin in Britain.

Muslims: Urdu is the major second language for Muslim Panjabi speakers (of Pakistani origin); it is a symbol of their national identity, it is their first language of literacy, and it is the language in which most discussion or teaching on the subject of Islam and related cultural matters takes place.

Urdu plays a broadly similar role for Muslim Gujarati speakers (of Indian origin). However, for this community the first language of literacy is Gujarati itself, and Gujaratis educated in post- Independence India will also have acquired literacy in Hindi - the language symbolising their national identity.

Urdu for Muslims of Pakistani or Indian origin (not forgetting those who first migrated to East Africa or elsewhere) is thus far more than what is normally understood by the term 'second language'. That is to say, Urdu is not merely a medium of communication with other groups, supplementing the mother tongue. It is in fact something much more important even than the first language, which tends to be undervalued by its speakers. Urdu may even be felt to be the 'real' mother tongue (with 'mother' here having the sense found in the expression 'mother country', which refers to the national unit with which people want to express their affiliation).

For Muslim Bengali speakers from Bangladesh, on the other hand, Urdu has no special value. People who grew up and were educated before 1971 (i.e in the former East Pakistan) may at least have acquired literacy in Urdu, though Bengali never gave way to Urdu in any sphere of activity. This is not to say that Urdu may not be understood by Bengali speakers.

Hindus: Among the Gujarati and Panjabi speaking Hindus, Hindi has a second language function somewhat less conspicuous than that of Urdu among the Muslims. Gujarati speakers value highly their own language and their Gujarati identity. Hindi is their second language of literacy, their link with other Hindus and with all other communities of Indian origin, but for most purposes, including religion, they use Gujarati.

Panjabi-speaking Hindus (relatively few in number in Britain) have religious writings in various dialects of Hindi as well as Panjabi, and look to standard Hindi as their main medium of cultural expression. Hindi in the Devanagari script may be considered their primary language of literacy (though not necessarily the first in order of learning, as children educated in the post-1966 Panjab State will have first learned to read and write Panjabi in the Gurmukhi script.) In terms of mutual intelligibility, Panjabi is very close to Hindi (much more so than is Gujarati). Indeed, Hindu Panjabi speakers often mix Hindi and Panjabi in their everyday speech, making it difficult to identify which of the two languages a person is speaking at any given time.

Sikhs: For Sikh Panjabi speakers who were educated in India, Hindi will also be the main second language, being the national language of their country but having no special cultural or religious significance. Many older Sikhs have both Urdu and/or Hindi as additional languages of literacy.

In summary, although Hindi-Urdu is not native to many of the population of South Asian origin and parentage in Britain, it is clear that this language, in its two modes or styles, has a vital function as the language of intergroup communication between the different linguistic communities. It is the only language other than English through which communication may be effected with the South Asian community as a whole, which is why it is used by the BBC for the Sunday morning radio and television broadcasts. By contrast, Panjabi, Gujarati and Bengali languages, which are the mother tongues of larger numbers of people, are restricted in their usefulness to particular groups.

4. South Asian languages in the British context

4.1 Linguistic diversity and multilingualism

The Introduction to the book referred to the diversity of languages in the Indian Subcontinent. Even in Britain, with a population of South Asian origin estimated at just over one million, there are the five major languages dealt with in the previous chapter, plus several other languages (e.g. Marathi, Tamil) spoken here by much smaller numbers of people, together with several categories of dialect for many of these languages.

What is too rarely considered is the number of common elements which permeate this diversity - the shared patterns of linguistic structure and the shared resources of vocabulary. These greatly facilitate mutual intelligibility between speakers of different languages, or at least make it easier for people to learn each others' languages. Some of the common ground in the area of grammar and sounds has already been described in Chaper 2. With vocabulary, too, the enormous number of words borrowed from external sources constitute a kind of common pool or bank from which speakers of each language can draw to express common meanings. In this way large numbers of borrowed Persian and Arabic words are shared by speakers of many languages, particularly Muslims, and the same is true of Sanskrit words for Hindus. Moreover, as in the case of all former British colonial territories, English vocabulary forms an indispensable and fully naturalised part of South Asian languages. (Just how naturalised these words have become is shown by the fact that they are written in the various South Asian scripts in a way which represents not their British but their South Asian pronunciation.)

An important factor increasing the 'common ground' between languages is the process of convergence referred to in section 2.2, whereby unrelated languages in contact with each other in multilingual situations can influence each other in respect of grammatical structure and sounds, as well as in the matter of vocabulary loans. This process has been found to occur in the British context, too, in a study of the mutual influences of English and Panjabi in the speech of Sikh children in Leeds (see Note 6, p 47). It was found to be quite common for speakers to switch from one language to the other several times within a single sentence: this gives the impression of a mixed or 'hybrid' language. There is often a good reason underlying such cases of language switch, and the mixed language which results need not be regarded as 'inferior' in any way to either of the languages contributing to it.

The willingness of people to use languages or dialects other than their own, however imperfectly, is a major factor serving to reduce the potential problems of linguistic diversity. Thus, speakers of the various local dialects in South Asia will be familiar at least with their regional language, and most people, of whatever language, will be able to make some use of Hindi-Urdu, even if only in terms of understanding but not speaking. This reflects the centuries-old propensity for bi- and multi-lingualism on the part of the people of the Subcontinent (see Note 7, p 47), and in particular the use of 'Hindustani' as a lingua franca dating from the 16th century.

All of this tends to suggest that the notorious diversity of South Asian languages may be more apparent than real, certainly as far as the communities in Britain are concerned.

4.2 Maintenance of the languages in schooling and communications

In contrast to the general characteristic of people of South Asian origin to have wide linguistic repertoires, the indigenous population of this country, apart from the Celtic areas, is solidly mono-lingual. (This is despite the fact of the several 'linguistic inva-sions' of the British Isles, ending with the Norman Conquest, and the many external influences on the development of the English lan-guage.) This linguistic ethnocentricity of the host population and its corresponding suspicion of bilingualism may well affect the degree to which South Asian languages are successfully maintained in Britain. The pressure to assimilate to the majority culture here is in marked contrast to the situation in multilingual areas such as Malaysia and East Africa, where South Asian emigrants have succeeded in maintaining their linguistic identity.

Schooling

Nevertheless, a large number of children of South Asian parentage attend community-organised mother-tongue classes outside their nor-mal school hours, which testifies to the determination of these com-munities to pass on their languages to later generations. (See Note 8, p 47 for sources of information on these classes.) For example, a recent survey of the use of Asian languages in Leicester found that 95% of parents of South Asian origin sampled felt it important for children to learn an Asian language (see Note 9, p 47).

Much of the work of such mother-tongue classes is concerned with teaching the children to read and write. This is because literacy in the community language, rather than oral skills, is of paramount im-portance to many people of South Asian origin; a person is not felt to know a language unless he or she has mastered the script. This is linked with the high regard in which script and calligraphic arts are held in Asian societies, in contrast to the Western attitude which values highly the typed or printed word. The connection between choice of script and religious affiliation, discussed with reference to Panjabi (3.1) and Urdu and Hindi (3.4 and 3.5), is another manifestation of the function of literacy skills (see Note 10, p 47).

In the state school sector, the opportunity to take GCE 'O' and 'A' levels and CSE (Mode 3) in some South Asian languages (particularly Urdu, Panjabi and Gujarati) is available in an increasing number of schools. However, the possibility that the teaching of community languages will be incorporated on a much wider basis in the school curriculum has been brought somewhat nearer by the coming into force (in July 1981) of the EEC Directive on the education of migrant workers' children, which requires statutory provision of mother-tongue teaching (see Note 11, p 47). In anticipation of the requirements of the Directive, the Department of Education and Science funded an experiment into bilingual infant education (the 'Mother Tongue and English Teaching' Project conducted in Bradford - see Note 12, p 48), and set up the Linguistic Minorities Project in the Institute of Education, London University, which looked into the nature and extent of bilingualism in England (see Note 13, p 48).

To help meet the demand for teaching materials in minority languages, the former Schools Council conducted a curriculum design project for Bengali teaching (together with Modern Greek) at primary level, and was involved in designing a new style of 16-plus examination for Hindi and Urdu (also Modern Greek) in the context of the development of multicultural curricula (see Note 14, p 48). Further, an increasing number of LEAS are appointing advisers or co-ordinators for mother-tongue or community-language teaching. Yet another development in this direction was the setting up in 1980, by the National Congress of Languages in Education, of a Working Party to look at language diversity and its implications for schools and LEAS. The Working Party report makes substantial recommendations on the future role of minority languages in mainstream education (see Note 15, p 48).

Besides recognising the proven educational advantages of developing a child's mother tongue side by side with the language in which most schooling takes place (i.e English), all these developments are aimed at promoting a greater respect for languages other than English in the British context, and a wider appreciation among the population as a whole of the cultural and educational values of bilingualism.

Communications

As means of communication in the public arena, South Asian languages, like those of other linguistic minorities, are not greatly in evidence at present. BBC provision, on the national networks, is limited to a radio request programme for South Asian film music and a television magazine programme (both broadcast on Sunday mornings), and a midweek daytime television programme. These are all in Hindi-Urdu. A particular BBC TV programme on mother-tongue teaching ('Languages for life') has been dubbed into Bengali and Panjabi (and Italian) and was transmitted in these languages in early 1984. Channel 4 has frequently broadcast South Asian films with original soundtrack (Hindi-Urdu) and English subtitles. Locally, certain radio stations also give a small amount of air time to broadcasts in minority languages (see Note 16, p 48).

A small number of publications by governmental and other public agencies are translated into South Asian languages. Examples include the instruction sheet accompanying the 1981 census, together with translations of all the census questions, and the material produced by the Stop Rickets Campaign. The BBC translated the support material for its 'Speak for Yourself' television series, though a follow-up study revealed that the translated versions were not distributed effectively among the communities who might have benefited from them. Information leaflets on a variety of subjects have been translated into minority languages, for example those on health and family planning, displayed in clinics (see Note 17, p 48).

In some areas South Asian interpreters are employed by public bodies, e.g. for hospital and clinic work, or for court proceedings (see Note 18, p 48). Some advice centres which deal with immigration problems can call on volunteer interpreters for minority languages. Such provision is far from adequate and does not accurately reflect the multilingual nature of this country's population (see Note 19, p 48).

The provision in public libraries of novels and other literature in minority languages is one small way for a local authority to recognise the fact of cultural and linguistic diversity among its rate-payers. In some (but by no means all) areas of high South Asian settlement libraries do indeed cater generously for the reading needs of linguistic minority adults and children (see Note 20, p 48).

Among the minorities themselves, the languages have wider functions stretching beyond the sphere of family and neighbourhood. A large number of newspapers and periodicals are produced in this country in minority languages; they are mainly weekly or monthly publications, but some appear daily (such as the Urdu 'Daily Jang', of many years standing). An information sheet compiled by the Commission for Racial Equality on the ethnic minority press lists the following totals of regular publications in South Asian languages: Bengali (11), Urdu (10), Panjabi (5), Gujarati (3), Hindi (2) and Telugu (1). As for the cultural activities, such as poetry symposia and other literary gatherings, and performances in music, dance and drama, which are organised by the communities and which take place

in the medium of their own languages - these are far too numerous
and varied to describe here (see Note 21, p 48).

As religion and language are intimately bound together for all linguistic minorities of South Asian origin, it is clear that maintenance of the language is not just a reflection of nostalgia or
sentimentality which will fade in time. Rather, it is central to
preserving the integrity of people's beliefs and value systems, and
is a major component in the maintenance of ethnic identity (see Note
22, p 49).

Concluding remarks

The purpose of this book has been to describe the major South Asian languages used in Britain, putting them into perspective vis-à-vis one another and against their South Asian background. It is outside the present scope to discuss the educational advantages to the individual of being bilingual, or to suggest that widespread bilingualism is a valuable resource to a community or a country. These are topics on which there is no shortage of research or debate worldwide.

Suffice it for the present to point to the following startlingly obvious, yet mostly ignored, fact. In several areas of Britain there live communities of people using South Asian languages, including the official languages of three major South Asian countries with which Britain has historical connections going back 200 years, plus two important regional languages of India. These are languages which have long-established literary traditions, and are important media for communication with very large numbers of people. (One fifth of the world's population lives in the Indian Subcontinent.) Moreover, these languages are spoken side by side with English in British streets and school playgrounds (see Note 23, p 49). In such areas they would make a very appropriate extension to the modern language curriculum for children of all linguistic backgrounds, including the indigenous native-speakers of English. They are certainly no less suitable than French, which is at present the main (almost the sole) modern language taught in schools, but which most children have little or no contact with, and little prospect of making any use of outside the classroom.

The multicultural nature of this society is gradually being reflected in school curricula and examination syllabuses. Surely South Asian languages will have a considerable part to play in this development.

Appendix I

Indo-European correspondences

Sounds: Some examples of sound correspondences between Hindi and English were quoted in section 1.2 (p 5ff). They are stated here more fully.

In the table below, corresponding words are shown from languages representing four branches of the Indo-European language family, including classical languages, of two to three thousand years' antiquity, and modern languages. They are: Romance (Latin and French); Greek (Classical Greek); Indo-Aryan (Sanskrit and Hindi); Germanic (English).

	Latin	French	Greek	Sanskrit	Hindi	English
1a)	pater	père	pater	pitā	pitā	father
b)	ped-	pied	pod-	pāda	pãv	foot
2a)	tres	trois	treis	traya	tīn	three
b)	tu	tu	tu	tvam	tū	thou
3a)	duo	deux	duo	dva	do	two
b)	decem	dix	deka	dasha	das	ten

Explanation:

1: Many words of the same (or similar) meaning begin with the sound 'p' in the Romance, Greek and Indo-Aryan branches, while the corresponding words in the Germanic branch begin with the sound 'f'. This 'equation', i.e. 'Latin p = Greek p = Sanskrit p = Germanic f, at the beginning of words' can be stated with the force of law; indeed, these examples form part of Grimm's Law, named after one of the 19th century philologists who established such inter-language correspondences.

2: Similarly: 'Latin, Greek and Sanskrit t = Germanic th, at the beginning of a word'.

3: 'Latin, Greek and Sanskrit d = Germanic t.' This is also exemplified by the second consonant of the words in 1b above.

Grammar: The 'sister' relationship of Sanskrit to Latin and Greek is quite evident in the realm of grammar, too. Like the two classical languages of Europe, Sanskrit is highly inflected: anyone who has enjoyed learning the 'tables' of word endings (inflections) in Latin and/or Greek might not feel too daunted by the task of mastering

Sanskrit grammar, which has a more complex pattern of inflexions. For example, Sanskrit has three genders in nouns (masculine, feminine and neuter, like both Latin and Greek); three 'numbers' in nouns and verbs (singular, dual and plural, as in Classical Greek but not Latin); and eight 'cases' in nouns (nominative, accusative, etc, compared with 6 in Latin and 5 in Classical Greek).

This extra complexity for a learner of Sanskrit is somewhat compensated by the fact that some of the endings themselves have the same phonetic shape as those of Latin and Greek. (This is of course further evidence for the genetic relationship between the languages.) For example, the sounds 'm', 's' and 't' are typical components of Sanskrit and Latin verb endings in the 1st, 2nd and 3rd persons respectively (i.e. I, thou, he, she or it), e.g. Sanskrit: abharam, abharas, abharat (I etc carried) and Latin: ferebam, ferebas, ferebat (same meaning). (Despite their somewhat dissimilar phonetic shape, the roots of this verb in the two languages, bhar- and fer- respectively, have a common ancestry too.)

Appendix II

The language families of the Indian Subcontinent

The four language families of the Indian Subcontinent are, in increasing order of numbers of speakers, Sino-Tibetan, Austro-Asiatic,
Dravidian, and the Indo-Aryan branch of Indo-European. (Detailed
reference works on South Asian languages are named in Note 24,
p 49.)

1. Sino-Tibetan. These languages are spoken by less than 1% of the
population of the Subcontinent. Their speakers are Mongoloid-type
people, of the Himalayan regions. One of the most important of these
languages numerically is Manipuri, with about 500,000 speakers in
the Indian State of Manipur, which borders on Assam (India) and
Burma. Languages of this family were once widespread over South
Asia, especially before the advent of speakers of Indo-Aryan languages. Other members of this language family, located outside the
Subcontinent, are Chinese, Tibetan and Burmese.

2. Austro-Asiatic. These languages are spoken by a little over 1% of
the population of the Subcontinent, though like the Sino-Tibetan
group they were once much more widespread. They have survived in the
hill and forest regions of Central and Eastern India, on the
Himalayan slopes and on the Nicobar Islands; their speakers are
Austroloid-type people. An important subgroup of this language
family are the Munda languages, of which one, Santali, has about 3
million speakers in parts of Orissa, Bihar and West Bengal States.
Externally, Austro-Asiatic languages include Khmer (Kampuchea) and
Vietnamese.

3. Dravidian. This family includes the major languages of South
India, with about 20% of the population of the Subcontinent (i.e
about 140 million speakers). Dravidian peoples are thought to have
prehistoric connections with Asia Minor and the Eastern Mediter-
ranean; they were the dominant population throughout the Indian Subcontinent before the coming of the Indo-European speaking people
(the Indo-Aryans). The ancient civilisations of the Panjab and Sind,
based on Harappa and Mohenjo-daro respectively, are considered to be
Dravidian, though the scripts associated with these cities have yet
to be deciphered.

Dravidian languages gave way to Indo-Aryan in the Northern and
Central parts of the Subcontinent, with a few pockets remaining such
as Brahui (300,000 speakers in Baluchistan, Pakistan), but are
firmly established in the south of India and in northern Sri Lanka.
Some of these languages can boast long literary traditions: documen-
tary evidence for the ancestors of three of the major Dravidian lan-

guages, Tamil, Telugu and Kannada, dates back to about 500 A.D. These three languages, together with Malayalam, constitute four of the fifteen languages recognised by the Indian Constitution. (There are no known relationships between the Dravidian family and languages spoken outside South Asia.)

4. Indo-Aryan. This is a major branch of the Indo-European family of languages. Indo-Aryan languages are spoken by about 75% of the population of the Subcontinent (about 520 million speakers). 11 of the 15 languages recognised by the Indian Constitution are Indo-Aryan: Assamese, Bengali, Gujarati, Hindi, Kashmiri, Marathi, Oriya, Panjabi, Sanskrit, Sindhi and Urdu. Indo-Aryan languages are located exclusively within the Subcontinent. Outside, the most closely related branch of Indo-European is that of the Iranian languages (e.g. Modern Persian). (As this book is largely concerned with particular Indo-Aryan languages, no more information need be noted here.)

Appendix III

Further features of the grammar of verbs in Indo-Aryan languages

(This supplements the information given in 2.2.I)

a)   In the past tense of transitive verbs (i.e. verbs which take an object), a construction is used which resembles the English passive rather than active formulation. (Thus: "the bread was eaten by Ram" (passive) compared with the active "Ram ate the bread".) The verb agrees with its object, rather than its subject, in number and gender.

e.g. rām ne   roṭī   khāī
     Ram (by)* bread (was) eaten
     Ram ate the bread

*This is a special postposition indicating the 'agent' in this type of construction.

N.B. Bengali is exceptional among the languages described in this book in that it uses an active-type construction in the past tenses of transitive verbs.

b)   The use of 'compound verbs' is very common in the Indo-Aryan languages. These consist of a verb in its 'root' form (i.e. with no inflexions), which indicates the main part of the meaning of the compound, followed by another verb, which is inflected normally, which somewhat modifies the meaning of the first verb.

e.g. i)   non-compound verb:

     rājindar ne apnī kitābẽ becī
     Rajinder * his   books   (were) sold

     Rajinder sold his books

(* see a) above on transitive past tenses)

     ii) compound verb:

     rājindar ne apnī kitābẽ bec ḍālī

     Rajinder   his   books   sell (were) done some-
                                       thing drastic

     Rajinder sold off (got rid of, went and sold) his books.

NB. The second verb in a compound has an independent meaning when used alone; the verb d̠āl, from the above example, usually means 'put'. In a compound, its meaning will vary according to the verb it is paired with.

Such constructions can best be compared with the English idiomatic use of 'phrasal verbs' such as 'sell off', 'sell out', 'sell up', although the latter, unlike the Indo-Aryan compound verbs, are usually restricted to a colloquial style. Exact English translations for these compound verbs are often hard to find.

Appendix IV

Teaching materials for English-speaking learners of the languages dealt with in this book

Panjabi

SHACKLE, C: Teach yourself Punjabi. English Universities Press. 1972.

SHARMA, J N and S K Sharma: Punjabi as a second language (with tapes). The Language Centre, Hockley, Birmingham 1977.

Gujarati

LAMBERT, H M: Gujarati language course. Cambridge University Press. 1971.

Bengali

HUDSON, D F: Teach yourself Bengali. English Universities Press. 1965.

Urdu/Hindi

MCGREGOR, R S: Outline of Hindi grammar. 2nd edition. Oxford University Press. 1977.

RUSSELL R: A new course in Hindustani for learners in Britain. School of Oriental and African Studies (Extramural Division), University of London. Vols 1-4, 1980-82.

WEIGHTMAN, S C R: Introduction to Hindi for the VSO (with tapes). School of Oriental and African Studies (Extramural Division), University of London. 1979.

Scripts

LAMBERT, H M: Introduction to the Devanagari script. Oxford University Press. 1953.

RUSSELL, R: A new course in Hindustani for learners in Britain. Vol 4 of this course is wholly concerned with the Urdu script (see under Urdu/Hindi above for publication details).

Notes and references

1. Surveys of minority languages include:

Rosen, H and T Burgess: Languages and dialects of London school-children. Ward Lock Educational. 1980.

Inner London Education Authority. 1983 Language census. ILEA Document no. 916/83, 1983.

Linguistic Minorities Project, London University Institute of Education:
a) Linguistic minorities in England. The Report of the Linguistic Minorities Project submitted to the Department of Education and Science in July 1983. University of London Institute of Education. Distributed by Tinga Tinga, Heinemann Educational Books.

b) The other languages of England. Routledge and Kegan Paul. 1985.

2. The 1971 census data on the overseas-born population is discussed on a region-by-region basis in: Campbell-Platt, K: Linguistic minorities in Britain. Runnymede Trust. 1978.

3. Various approaches to the collection of statistical information on minority language communities are surveyed in: Reid, E: 'The Newer Minorities: Spoken Languages and Varieties.' In: Trudgill, P: Language in the British Isles. Cambridge University Press. 1984. This paper also puts present-day linguistic diversity in the Britsh Isles into its long-term historical context and discusses the educational and other implications of the 'local dialect' vs 'standard language' question which affects many South Asian (and other) communities in Britain.

A detailed description of the techniques applied and the problems encountered in locating respondents for a survey of language use is given in: Smith, G P: Locating populations of minority language speakers: an example of practice from the Coventry Language Project. Working Paper No.1, Linguistic Minorities Project, London University Institute of Education. 1982.

A major problem in language survey work is the lack of agreement on precise names for particular languages, with different speakers using different names to report the same language, or the same name for different languages. Difficulties in interpreting informants' responses to such questions as: "What is the name of the language

46

you speak at home?" are illustrated in: Smith, G P: The geography and demography of South Asian languages in England: some methodological problems. Working Paper No.2. Linguistic Minorities Project, London University Institute of Education. 1982. This paper gives sample results from large-scale surveys of schoolchildren in Coventry, Bradford, Peterborough and the London Borough of Haringey. Another investigation into the language naming question, as it relates to speakers of Panjabi, Urdu and Hindi, is reported in: Mobbs, M C: Language naming in surveys of South Asian communities. Newsletter of the National Council for Mother Tongue Teaching. Winter 1982.

4. The interpretation of language data in Indian censuses is dealt with from a historical point of view in Khubchandani, L: 'A demographic typology for Hindi, Urdu and Panjabi speakers in South Asia.' In: Language and society. McCormack, W C and S Wurm (eds). Mouton. 1979.

5. This investigation into the distinct identity (or otherwise) of Urdu and Hindi is described in: Mobbs, M C: 'Two languages or one? The significance of the language names 'Hindi' and 'Urdu'' In: Journal of Multilingual and Multicultural Development. 2,3. 1981.

6. For this study of the mixed English-Panjabi speech, see: Agnihotri, R K: Process of assimilation: a sociolinguistic study of Sikh children in Leeds. York University, unpublished D.Phil. thesis. 1979.

7. Multilingualism in India has been discussed by many scholars, for example: Pattanayak, D P: Multilingualism and mother-tongue education. Oxford University Press (Delhi). 1981.

8. Educational and political issues associated with mother-tongue teaching are dealt with in: Saifullah Khan, V: 'Provision by minorities for language maintenance.' In: Bilingualism and British education: the dimensions of diversity. Centre for Information on Language Teaching and Research. 1976; and: Martin-Jones, M: 'The Newer Minorities: Literacy and Educational Issues.' In: Trudgill, P (ed): Language in the British Isles. Cambridge University Press. 1984.

9. This survey is reported in: Wilding, J: Ethnic minority languages in the classroom: a survey of Asian parents in Leicester. Leicester City Council and Leicester Council for Community Relations. 1981.

10. These ideas relating to literacy are suggested in the paper by Martin-Jones referred to in Note 8.

11. The full text of the Directive is given in: Commission for Racial Equality: The EEC's directive on the education of children of

migrant workers: its implications for the education of children from ethnic minority groups in the U.K. 1980.

12. The Bradford infant bilingual project is described in: Rees, O A and B Fitzpatrick: Mother tongue and English teaching project: summary of the report. School of Research in Education, Bradford University. 1981.

13. The major publication from this project was referred to in Note 1. When its DES funding ceased, this project was succeeded in May 1983 by the ESRC-funded 'Community Languages in Education' project, also based at the University of London Institute of Education.

14. Proposals for a new 16+ examination in minority languages are described in: Broadbent, J et al: Community languages at 16+. Longmans/Schools Council. 1983.

15. See: Reid, E (ed.): Minority community languages at school, Report of the National Congress on Languages in Education Working Party. 1984. This report includes a discussion of relevant educational issues, a useful bibliography and an outline of recent and current research projects related to bilingual education in England.

16. The field of broadcasting in minority languages is surveyed in: Anwar, M: Who tunes in to what? A report on ethnic minority broadcasting. Commission for Racial Equality. 1978.

17. A catalogue of leaflets available in minority languages has been compiled by the National Association of Citizens Advice Bureaux and the Commission for Racial Equality: Community information: Asian languages directory. NACAB and CRE. 1980.

18. As an example, interpreting services in the Birmingham area are listed in: Plummer, J: Babel in Birmingham: a report on the provision of interpreting and translating services. AFFOR, 1 Finch Road, Birmingham 19. 1975.

19. These advice centres are catalogued in: Immigration casework with migrant workers: a directory of agencies offering help mainly in central London, compiled by the Migrant Services Unit of the London Voluntary Service Council. 1981.

20. This aspect of the library service is discussed in: Elliot, P: Library needs of children attending self-help mother-tongue schools in London. Polytechnic of North London. 1981.

21. See: Khan, N: The arts Britain ignores: the arts of ethnic minorities in Britain. Community Relations Commission (now Commission for Racial Equality). 1976.

48

22. The relationship between language and ethnicity has developed into an important research area within the field of social psychology. A representative collection of papers in this area is: Giles, H and B St. Jacques (eds): Language and ethnic relations. Pergamon Press. 1979.

23. Educational and other important aspects of one South Asian language which has taken root in Britain are discussed in: Russell, R (ed): Urdu in Britain. Urdu Markaz. 1982.

24. Reference works on South Asian languages include:

Hugoniot, R D: Bibliographical index of the lesser known languages of India and Nepal. Summer Institute of Linguistics, India and Nepal. 1970.

Breton, R J-L: Atlas géographique des langues et des ethnies de l'Inde et du Subcontinent. Laval. 1976.

The former is especially useful for language names, the latter for demographic statistics.